Sight

Written by Mandy Suhr

Illustrated by Mike Gordon

Wayland

The Senses

Hearing
Sight
Smell
Taste
Touch

This edition published in 1994 by
Wayland (Publishers) Limited

First published in 1993 by
Wayland (Publishers) Limited
61 Western Road, Hove
East Sussex, BN3 1JD

© Copyright Wayland (Publishers) Limited

Series Editor: Mandy Suhr
Book Editor: Francesca Motisi
Editorial Assistant: Zoe Hargreaves
Consultants: Jane Battell and Richard Killick

British Library Cataloguing in Publication Data
Suhr , Mandy
 Sight- (Senses series)
 I. Title II. Gordon , Mike III. Series
 612.8

Hardback ISBN 0-7502-0656-X

Paperback ISBN 0-7502-1408-2

Typeset by Wayland (Publishers) Limited
Printed and bound in Italy by Rotolito Lombarda S.p.A

Contents

Look around you, what can you see?

How many different colours
can you see?

How many different shapes
can you see?

You can see things that are very close.

You can see things that are far away.

You see things that make
you feel happy.

You see things that make you feel sad.

We use our eyes to see. Your eye is a bit like a camera. It works by letting light in from the world outside. Inside your eye is a lens, like the one inside a camera.

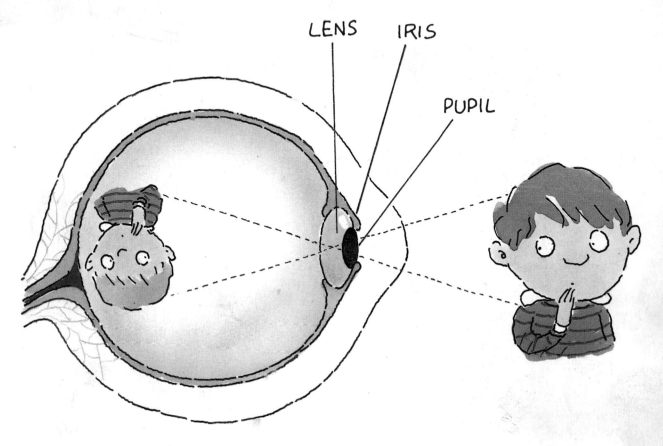

LENS   IRIS

PUPIL

The lens focuses the light to make a tiny picture at the back of your eye. This picture is upside down, just like in the camera. Your brain turns it the right way up for you.

At the back of your eyes are light detectors. They send messages to your brain along special pathways called nerves.

These messages tell your brain what your eyes are seeing.

The light goes into your eye through a special hole called your pupil. This is the black part of your eye.

The coloured part of your eye is called your iris.

This part is stretchy and makes the hole bigger when it is dark...

and smaller when it is sunny so just the right amount of light gets in.

Our eyes are protected by eyelids and eyelashes. They keep dust and dirt out of our eyes.

There are tiny holes at the corner of each eye. Salty water called tears comes from here to wash your eyes and keep them clean.

Some things are so small that they can only be seen properly if you look through a magnifying glass to make them bigger.

Sometimes they are so small that they can't be seen at all by your eyes. But if you look through a microscope you may be able to see them.

Being able to see is very useful.
It can stop you from hurting
yourself.

It can also help you
stop other people
being hurt.

watch out!

Some people's eyes don't work so well and they need some help to see properly. So they wear glasses like my brother, Jim.

Glasses make things clearer to see. The lenses in the glasses help the lenses in your eyes to focus properly.

Some people can't see at all. They have to use their other senses to help them get around.

My grandad uses a stick to feel his way around.

Some blind people have a dog who is specially trained to help them.

Both of our eyes point forward. If we want to see all around us we have to turn our heads.

But some animals have eyes on each side of their heads, like these rabbits. They can see all around them without turning their heads.

Some animals can see really well, even from a long way off. This eagle has very good eyesight, which helps it to catch its food.

28

You can see a long way just by using your eyes. But if you look through a telescope you will see even further! Try this for yourself and see how far you can see.

Notes for adults

The Senses is a series of first information books specially designed for the early stages of reading. Each book has a simple, factual text and amusing illustrations, combining reading for pleasure with fact-finding.

The content of the book addresses the requirements of the National Curriculum for Science, Key Stage One. The series takes a closer look at the human body, explaining very simply how we use each of our senses to learn about the world around us. This book explores the sense of sight.

1. Design experiments to test eyesight, such as distance tests (how far can you see?), range of vision (how far from side to side can you see without moving your head?), and size (what is the smallest text you can

read?). This activity promotes collaborative learning when carried out in small groups. It encourages discussion and hypothesizing, both important language skills. Children can also be encouraged to design ways to record their results.

2. Set up experiments where children can explore the effects of concave and convex lenses of varying thicknesses.

3. Make your own lens. Spread a piece of cling film over a roll of sticky tape. Drop a small amount of water into the centre. Hold it over a piece of text. Adjust the amount of water and tension of the cling film to find the best magnifying effect.

4. Explore various optical illusions.

Books to read

Sight, Sound and Signals by Julian Rowe

   (Oxford University Press, 1993)

Your Senses by Angela Royston (F. Lincoln, 1993)

Experiment With Senses by Monica Byles (Two-Can, 1992)

My Science Book of Senses by Neil Ardley

   (Dorling Kindersley, 1992)

Senses (Criss-Cross) by Hazel Songhurst (Wayland, 1993)

The Senses (Science in our World) by Peter D. Riley

   (Atlantic Europe Publishing Company, 1991)